"*Hackable Animal* offers a cry for help for a world under assault by environmental destruction and tech over-reliance. But this collection is also a call to arms. *Hackable Animal* is stunning in idea and execution. This is a one-of-a-kind collection for here and now. Ian Ramsey has created something beautiful.
—SEAN PRENTISS, author of *Finding Abbey,* winner of the National Outdoor Book Award

"These poems, compounded of humor and agony, awareness and disgust, awe and regret, take the fervent temperature of an overrun, going-fast, gizmo-ruined planet. The spirit that moves here is urgent for very good reasons that veer far beyond the latest eco-alarms. Ian Ramsey has done what poets traditionally have done—taken the grit and dirt into his mouth and spewed out poems that can reach the vast distances inside human beings. It's inspiring to meet an un-self-justifying poet who meets the exponential, ravening emptiness full-on in cascades and files of words that are terribly honest about the earth-hurt any sentient soul now feels."

—BARON WORMSER, author *Legends of the Slow Explosion*

"Ramsey guides his readers into an unnerving vision of our global moment. Many of these poems can be painful to read; Yet *Hackable Animal* won't let us accept doom as the answer. Again and again, Ramsey reminds us that this imperfect world is still an open door, a portal into spirit and nature, into self and community. In poem after poem, he flies us through terror and dismay, but he never submits to them. Instead, he gives us the gift that he gives to himself, in his paean to Edward Abbey: 'What hope he held for his charred soul. What hope I hold for mine.'"

—DAWN POTTER, author of *Accidental Hymn*

"Reading Ian Ramsey's intelligent poems about the elemental concern of environmental disaster, climate change, and the role human beings have as stewards of the natural world is to encounter a startling beauty that emerges from the anxiety of experience, even a yearning for innocence. Like his poetic ancestor, William Blake, Ramsey, too, never loses heart. But, these are genuinely American poems. They are breezy and lucid. They come out of the vernacular of everyday life. They are inventive and vigorous. What's more, Ramsey's moral imagination is always tethered to his true poetic gift."

— DAVID BIESPIEL, author of *Republic Cafe*

# HACKABLE ANIMAL

# HACKABLE ANIMAL

poems by

## IAN RAMSEY

**WAYFARER BOOKS**
WWW.WAYFARERBOOKS.ORG

Look for our titles in paperback, ebook, and audiobook wherever books are sold.
Wholesale offerings for retailers available through Ingram.

Wayfarer Books is committed to ecological stewardship.
We greatly value the natural environment and invest in conservation.
For each book purchased in our online store we plant one tree.

PO Box 1601, Northampton, MA 01061

860.574.5847 | info@homeboundpublications.com

HOMEBOUNDPUBLICATIONS.COM & WAYFARERBOOKS.ORG

*For Heidi*

# Contents

"The real problem of humanity is the following: We have Paleolithic emotions, medieval institutions and godlike technology."

—E.O. Wilson, *Harvard Magazine*


"In the first place you can't see anything from a car; you've got to get out of the goddamned contraption and walk, better yet crawl, on hands and knees, over the sandstone and through the thornbush and cactus. When traces of blood begin to mark your trail you'll begin to see something, maybe. Probably not."

—Ed Abbey, *Desert Solitaire*


"...we are no longer mysterious souls—we are now hackable animals."

—Yuval Noah Harari, Speech at Davos, 2020

# KICK

Just before dusk in the Peruvian Amazon, I'm sprinting,
chasing a flapping sphere across a muddy pitch swagged in
tight by sweaty rainforest. I pass and trap among men
who grew up in huts hunting monkeys and now work for
oil companies. Real Madrid Jerseys. Machetes on the ground.
We kick and trap, pass and cross, the corner kick's topspin
an unrehearsed path. The scuff and scrap ball is bouncing
among bodies, is wondering why we don't kick more cleanly,
why we don't notice the air hissing out by gasping millimeters;
even as it slides and bumps threadbare, this glorious wobble
that stitches together the whole operation is wondering
why it gets less attention than the Jaguar tracks downtrail,
or the new Reggaeton single we all sing, "son Tus Movimientos."
Downriver, the Mascho-Piro tribe knows nothing of metal tools.
A lowly schoolteacher, I know nothing of children or savings
after decades spent obsessed with travel, conniving grants and tickets,
hitching rides, missing weddings and drifting away from friends.
As I run backwards on an earth spinning forwards toward a ball
rolling sideways, the revolutions gather in my pulse, thumping.
Across the lumpy field, the booted ball launches, curling wide
of the goal, rising toward the sun's vapored fading. Following,
I wonder if I'm leaving or returning home. Offsides or on.

# SANDBAGS

Are
available
for free across
Broward County,
ahead of the hurricane.
The same sandbags that
my grandfather foxholed behind
in '44, Ardennes bullets strutting
violently across canvas. The wet sacks
that we slugged into the Caribbean Sea,
day after day, trying to rebuild a dying reef.
Mississippi. East China Sea. Bangladesh. Mosul
sandbagging IED blasts. There is one last Galapagos
tortoise who remembers the world before sandbags.
There are ten thousand villages sliding into the sea, leaking
and buttressed, waiting. They are putting the earth in bags and
trying to control it, a last-ditch wager. They are slopping stacks
around Miami Beach highrises, barricading marble infinity pools
and brushed steel appliances, zoning laws and insurance policies.
The ocean just sighs, rolls up its foamy sleeves, keeps right on coming.

# ABASHIRI

I aspire to end up glacier-frozen,
        or in a grizzly's gut, following
in the lapsed family tradition.
        Going back ten thousand years,
I mean. I'm thinking about this
        while eating wasabi peas beneath
a wooly mammoth in a museum
        in northern Japan.

The burly pachyderm,
        found in a ten-mile plank of ice,
is now a resin of chemicals,
        instead of a giant lung
of fresh-chewed ferns.
        I'm thinking about becoming
a glacier entrepreneur,
        cutting glaciers out of Greenland
and rigging them in South Beach
        for ice-age mojitos, glaciers
in Sāu Paolo for air conditioning,
        glaciers for the next big Dubai
figure skating complex where
        Korean teenagers can land
triple axels on a LEED-certified
        organic surface.

Since we can't hurl spears
        or love each other beneath
wads of furs, we'll glacier out

Singapore to host the winter Olympics,
recycling meltoff into bottled water
and using profits to support
a cooperative of vegan
climate-change activists
making artisan kombucha
from ferns found in mammoth stomachs.

Glacier off tops of mountains
and glacier them back on,
glacier oceans back to cooler temps,
glacier my Pleistocene instincts
to my paleo diet and write an app
that tracks the eskering in real time.

Popping another pea,
I look up, part-orphan,
part-ambition, considering
the noiseless shaggy requiem.
It doesn't look back.

# EXTINCTION: BOREDOM

The sense of missing out. The umwelt of urgency. The ad nauseum hours of click-click-click that ended in some rabbit hole of "How did I get here?" were more absence than presence even as they sought to avoid absence. One buzz or fifty pinged the compulsion of my pituitary veer, and the moment waded through the seductive frenzy like something else was always around the corner, some there there. Distracting headlines, distracting colors, the distracting sense that if I stopped clicking, I'd be faced with nothing. It was jackpots and blown-out neurotransmitters, every ding a sexy meteorite falling through the atmosphere of my soul, but, hey, what happens in my brain stays in my brain, baby. Any reprieve from the existential flatline was fired up, wired up, a beeping, buzzing bath of novelty, as I heard what else? in what had once been now, a breaking of truce between inner neurotic and the incessant whispering of existence. Where was my nearly thinking going? I'm still in the drivers seat, I told myself, even as each moment hung more cravings on my hippocampus, each moment sliding away and eroding like beach sand that is beading more and more plastic each moment.

# FIRE

Ojai's on fire and the San Juans are on fire
and the southern Amazon's on fire, just like
      Myanmar,
all visible on a world map with little flame
emojis on my phone, an effort by
a well-meaning NGO to gamify the burning
of our world. Gamify: a strange response
to thousand-year-old villages vaporizing,
the screams of mothers digitized, beamed
to satellites and cell towers, and thoughtful
Starbucksing thumbs noticing between
Instagram posts, holding the burning world
in their hands, gaining points for paying attention.
But threatening and cajoling and celebrating
and guilting are weaker than swiping,
      always swiping.
Swipe and burn and swipe and melt and swipe
and terrorize and swipe and huddle in boats
in the Aegean and swipe for the dopamine drip.
In Portland it was 110 degrees, the Cascades burning.
I saw a photo of Gifford Pinchot and wondered
what he would think. Forest service planes floated
through the smoke like ghosts of fire seasons past.
On CNN, everything was burning, a cartoon of disaster.
The fire, persistent and lonely, keeps to itself and says:
"Here's a tree that is burning and here's a house
that is burning, even though water is nearby.
Yes, this dog is also burning, and when
will you wake up and start calling me by your name?"

# REFUGIA

I went to the trees again. Unable to grok the brunt
of the latest tweets about Greenlandic melt,
I hunkered under the storm-beaten tonnage
of autumn maples, trying to pilfer a minor league peace.
Help me. Salve me. The usual tropes for trees
when people are painful. Even the Sox in the playoffs
was a meager balm. Landwrecked, I gaped up
 at a thousand foliage fires ripping open the blue sky,
trying to imagine mapleless New England.
But in this capsized weather, things lean vagrant.
At the Vermont sugaring conference, a scientist said
there would be few maples in a century, and maybe
we should think about tapping birches. Had we savvied
the glycemic index of southern magnolias, or kudzu?
The wool-clad sugar farmers twisted their gray mustaches,
their children long gone to Boston and Atlanta,
where rush-hour traffic doesn't allow for much in the way
of silviculture but WiFi is considered a human right.
          Two hundred miles north,
the rare deep-soiled valley with south-facing slopes says
I'll take this sugar maple and that fern and those grasses
but there's no place for that birch. The rest of you
will have to make it over the next mountain range. Best of luck.
No matter that you outlasted the dinosaurs,
that ten million generations have broken their backs,
only for you to run aground.  You long for the old cohort
of more-or-less seasons. But here you are, ferocious and bony,
half-rooted in a strange latitude with a weather

that never quite arrives. Regardless, you perseverate,
hurling winged seeds into the weirding, your fate wobbling,
knuckleballish. But you've been here before a few times.
It's the top of the seventh. Or maybe the bottom of the ninth?
The Omaha Stormchasers versus the Lake Elsinore Storm. Play Ball.

# THE TWENTY-FIRST CENTURY

We had wanted to play Bill Monroe but our Chinese festival hosts insisted on "Call Me Maybe." Across the street, yesterday's five-story building was gone, replaced by the frame of a ten-story building in twenty hours. We soundchecked on the same stage that would soon host Kenny G, K-pop, and five thousand red-kerchiefed elementary children reciting "To struggle for the cause of communism, be prepared!" Exhausted from a week of gigs, pandas and fried duck, I had fallen asleep in the green room, dreaming of the village on the Ecuador-Colombia border where we looked unsuccessfully for last patches of intact rainforest. The police at the checkpoint interrogated us, worried about the recent narco bombing. Along the Mira River, black-skinned children asked us if we wanted to buy the four-foot-long endangered green iguana that they kept in a garbage can, before throwing up gang signs and rapping Jay Z's "Got plenty hoes because we getting that money my nigga." I woke to Chengdu kids rapping along to Eminem, and then it was time to get on stage. Then get on the bus. Then get on the plane to Beijing. I would miss most of the Forbidden City on the phone with an expat -ex -Navy Seal -water filtration dealer -who was finding instruments for us but mostly wanted to talk about bitcoin. After our gig, the next day we would rush through the Summer Palace, but miss the Great Wall because our flight was changed due to "Climate Adjustments." After fourteen hours of watching Bollywood and Avatar we landed in Newark, the last flight before Hurricane Sandy shut down the airport. We drove all night on the front edge of the storm, singing Bill Monroe to stay awake: "Keep me driving with a worried mind."

# EXTINCTION

I sat all morning in the Juneau airport,
flight delayed. Hake-bound halibuters,
Fairbanks firefighters, and cruise-shippers.

Float planes swarmed the Mendenhall Glacier's
foggy gist, the blue-shouldered cold forgetting
how ice once gathered up many more acres.

The cowboy talked loudly about moose hunting
five steps in front of the taxidermied polar bear,
the formaldehyde menace, up on two legs

and posed in a growl through a hundred photos
—these Beijing teens, that Arkansas minister—
At least the twelve-foot historical footnote

won't see the last survivors of her species
fade away in air-conditioned zoos, slowly
unfastening their tribe from the future.

But then, surely, the final moments of the last
woolly mammoth were no walk in the park,
alone on Wrangel Island's windy tussocks,

except for a dozen men with spears circling.
Who can say what it means when a million years
of evolution shatters its own mirror? The senator

casts the deciding budget vote that will save
the Hawaiian bird species or won't. Maybe.
The scientist who studied the bird for decades

is also extincted, left to elbow out her final years
as an EPA administrator in a changing climate
of divestment regs and emission negotiations.

But this morning I wake a world away from Juneau.
It's rainy season here in the mountains of Ecuador,
the nation with the most species near extinction.

Sapphire-vented pufflegs, glossy flower-piercers,
and mutable rain frogs that rearrange their skin.
Blue morphos. Drought. Spectacled bears. Logging.

No one said biodiversity was easy. As poets, we'd
rather die out leading our people through a forest
weeping with absinthe fire, or singing as a tsunami

gathers the sorrows of a thousand black fishes
against the sky. Instead, geneticists sequence
DNA to de-extinct flocks of passenger pigeons,

bioengineer coral reefs, fill logged jungles with
Zika-less mosquitoes buzzing the slash-and-burn
among herds of patented low-methane cows .

Here in the cloudforest, at sunrise's prelude,
the moss-laden groves shrug off sleep, inhaling
the fragile fog, ten thousand orchids rejoicing

at the seeping light. Amethyst-throated sun angels
spark and flick toward the promise of a new day,
one likely to pluck away yet another feather,

yet another egg. Even here, swaddled in densest
diversaphony, each missing branch or chirp
conjures tributaries of the disappeared,

and I wonder why I'm so obsessed with listening
for the single cricket that's not there.

# CARBON IS THE OPENED HEART

Crusoed for weeks now,
we took the washed-up plastics and made altars to the polar ice caps,
dancing open-loined around the ultraviolet
bottles that floated up
every day.

The fraying, faded yellow ropes
were polystyrene, the red frags were BPA,
the blueish bags a PVC that time washed off everything—the palm trees,
the deflated life raft,
the fluxing of the tide.

We played Pictionary,
you asking me what two words spell "extinction"
and I carved "fossil fuels"
in the Club Med sand, a hurricane by another name.

Slovenly with instinct,
we swam storm-lathed waves,
played tag, except that "it" kept changing
from paradise lost to paradise found
to fucking like it was the last night on earth.
We wore a crater in the plastiglomerate
and opened up the hours
like a can of rationed beans,
unfurled our bodies across each other,
briny and pounding with the night's combustion,
even as we imagined
flying away the next morning on the contrails.

Satellites blinked circles
in the glassy distances, but we spun to a different music,
        mutinied from the bluetoothed pathologies.


        We were extinctionaire seasteaders of the plasticene,
self-selected incubants of evolution,
            seeking not immortality, nor rocketed escape,
but to go down with the ship being the earth being pranks of possibility.

And what about the hundred-year typhoons rolling in every few weeks?

        It was a sequestered garden of sorts to take care of,
        a way to keep each other
            afloat even as the sea rose,
to help us swallow the sticky retinas of invasive fruit,
        to carve our names in the sand and hold each other.

To sink or swim.

# SMOKEY

The bear coughs the bristlecone smoke like the rest of us,
but isn't allowed into the visitors' center for AC and free Kool-Aid.
No one said it was easy being an icon, a t-shirt, an ad campaign.
And what can I learn from the bear? He wears a GPS ear tag
and I an iphone as I sit alone for two days in smoky Yosemite,
an abandoned husband with a burning heart. Half Dome
is more Beijing smog than Ansel Adams gelatin print wilderness.
Across the Sierras the Smokey signs feel useless. Endless helicopters
drop dispersant. The bear and I see extinction out of the corners
of our eyes. The annual fires roaring across the west are extinction
and administration's selling off public lands is extinction,
the last Grizzly  in the Sierras was once extinction, the cougar
crossing the highway a protest of extinction. The story ends
with the real Smokey sleeping out his days in D.C.'s National Zoo,
dreaming of sagebrush  while retirees eat weiners, and point.
A boy grows up, his head dreaming on a teddy bear. Without realizing it,
his life is a shrine to bears. Bears in Alaska. Bears in Hokkaido.
Bears in the Andes. Bears in Quebec. Bears that don't promise
self-actualization or a good 401K or freedom from cancer.
Bears that knock around the soul without permission.
Bears that ruin a marriage. The boy becomes a man who wants
to love women, but they will never smell like bears. People are people
but bears are a secret howling ladder to a world of smoky caves.
Even as I try not to think about bears, Smokey ambles slowly away,
his fur wet with my dreams. I have no right to bring him back to life.

# TO HAYDEN CARRUTH

The Costa Rican luxury suite had a view of the Pacific
but lacked rusting tools. Even in Anglesey, surrounded
by Neolithic ruins, the cottage plates were stacked too neatly.
As our plane raced to Seoul to avoid Fukushima's poisons,
I dreamed of black flies and fishers screaming in the night.
This is why I hide in the woods and listen to the earth.
Isn't that why you spent all those years in that Vermont
cowshed, reeking of pipe smoke, bar oil and hay?
When I can understand the animals, I will no longer need
people. Then I will write the earth's greatest poem.
It will be read by coyotes and goldfinches in a
logged-over clearing at sunrise on the longest day
of the year. Last night I drank two bottles of red wine
and looked at photos of the Alberta Tar Sands,
a watershed larger than Vermont. In deer season
the woods shake with guns. The cows shudder and,
just as you did, I bide my time.

# PARAMO

The katabatic wind screams down from the glaciers on Chimborazo,
Cotopaxi and Cayambe. This ice will be gone in a decade. The sky sleets,
blazes, rainbows and hails, all in a windy hour under the ozoneless glare.
The Quechua miners with sunblasted face drink beer in the camp.
I am with them, watching *The Matrix* in Spanish. I am trying to imagine
what a high-altitude villager without running water thinks of Neo's
virtual reality conundrum, but the fight scenes are really good.
At dinner I try to ask a miner about futbol but Spanish is a second language
for both of us. He worries about his five children while I worry about writing
the perfect poem. When I wake up in the middle of the night and stagger
out to pee at 13,000 feet, the Southern Cross is ringing with clarity and so is
my confusion. My sea-level lungs grasp at air. Last week, five thousand feet
down in the city, I watched a group of women dance a routine to Beyonce's
"All the Single Ladies," their Nikes and American Eagle shirts bright songbirds
of color against the pale adobe of a 500-year old Spanish Church.
On my Iphone news of Trump's solar tariffs dinged, and the Glaciers shrugged.
The older indigenous ladies walked by carrying bundles of sticks on their backs.
Once again, I feel far from home. Once again, my facebook status doesn't know
who I am despite what I tell the world. On the bus to Vilcabama I will tell the driver
to stop and I will get off and walk into the mountains, which remain aloof to my suffering.
Nevertheless, I am still breathing and a million grasses dance in the Andean wind.
They are the souls of all of the people and animals who have lived here. Their lives
are a bottomless well into which I lower myself, trying to drink, not to drown.

# THE NARROW ROAD TO THE INTERIOR

I wanted to hush the grief so I picked up Basho,
but the radio still chattered about the marathon bombings.
I wanted to hush the grief so I picked up Basho again,
but the watershed newsletter was lying there shouting
to call my senator about the proposed dam. I made a fire,
using the newsletter, and fell asleep. When I woke
I still wanted Basho. I looked through the window at the dense forest,
thinking of the wolf that a biologist friend had seen
up near the Quebec border, the supposedly extinct
mountain lions that a dozen friends had seen over the years.
I wanted to read about the famous pine at Takekuma.
Finally picking up my thumbed-over copy of Basho, I opened to
*Everywhere between pines graves, bringing home the fact*
*that even vows of "wing and wing, branch and branch,*
*forever merging" must also come to such, sadness increasing.*
I stepped outside into night's blue edge, a fisher screaming,
two owls hooting. Sweet reek of maple bud and pine sap.
Lynx and chipping sparrows moved north across the eastern forest.

# REINTRODUCTION

Wolves: the fugitive omen, founders of Rome,
the scourge of Red Riding Hood. Save them from
the hunters who say that hunting is conservation
until it might mean fewer elk. Save them from

the chuckle-puppet environmentalists in Boulder,
the ranchers speaking out of both sides of their subsidies,
the biologists speaking in carefully worded statistics,
the activists using ballot-box biology to reintroduce them.

The wolf howls deep in my brainstem, trotting through
the Pittman-Robertson Act, the subtleties of Yellowstone
trophic cascades, the jokes about *shoot, shovel, shut up*
that livestock operators are making. I'm wondering

if we love or fear wolves because we can't talk with them
more intimately than we can't talk with the earth
and the whole time there's this limbic echo of predators,
people telling stories of bloody sheep or the wild sanctity

of wolf habitat but mostly crying wolf or crying anti-wolf,
to feel worthy of words like *stewardship* and *heritage*
or at least to explain this wolf-shaped hole that we all
stand around, throwing coins into and making wishes.

There's a grainy nineteenth century photo, of Edwin Carter,
a Breckenridge taxidermist and naturalist, beside a dead lobo
well over six feet, surrounded by hundreds of stuffed bison,
elk, and a sign: *Don't Touch the Animals.*

You can see, behind Carter's Wyatt Earp mustache,
a quiet pride. You can see that he loves and fears
and hates and admires and has no idea that every
Colorado wolf will be gone in half a century.

The smoke from his cigar trails into the air, drifting
noose-like around the thick fur. How we all tentatively
circle these unknowable gods in wolf's clothing,
half killing, half preserving, half worshiping.

# CHANTEUSE

*For Concha Buika, Cantaora*

Blocks from Fenway, between old brickish streets,
college bars and start-ups, Concha Buika sings.
On Comm Ave, a Bruins bro *Fuck you's* a yellow cab
racing to beat the Tip O'Neill Tunnel's 9p.m. closing,
but onstage Buika starves the clocks, her voice
a salty dusk rustling in moon-dry creek bottoms,
her Roma rasp spattering the crowd like paint
or surf or tears, an urgent, orphaned longing.

All around this bridged-up city, built on fill,
the ocean crouches, waiting. And onstage,
Concha sings a hundred storms, born in Africa,
Iberia-sharpened, charging across the rising Atlantic,
tearing up old cartographies. Conakry a red puddle,
Madrid a dusty yellow wash. Hurricanes race,
their chords relentlessly spinning the seas feral,
heating and catalyzing an impulsive chemistry.

Across town, Kennedy School fellows debate the causes
of Syrians in Italy, Bangledeshis flooding Dhaka,
just as Buika's Bulerias equal India via Iberia
divided by suffering, an algorithm scaling up
across the Aegean and the Rio Grande as parched
south floods north, as we coil and stomp to Buika's
Afro-Cuban duende, trying to forget the bombed
marathoners still haunting the street outside.

And Buika —shadow-waisted with claves and fandango—
howls the new diaspora, singing "Vivir sin Miedo,"
her weeping and uprooted tides unlocking the distances.
Dogs or kin? The brunt of the question draws tight
as the hour lags, dizzy with strange weather.
I'll bet on the dark horse: the complex parable
read in the ancestor's chicken bones. Forget the maps.
We're following the seas, wherever they go.

# MAXIMON

The houses sinkholed into the earth and collapsed in on themselves and the six children inside whom I didn't know died, wearing hand-me-down Ronaldinho jerseys and dresses, with sticks of gum in their pockets. I walked the steep cobblestone streets where some of the 50,000 had "disappeared" a generation ago, and walked the market past bloody flanks of goat and racks of designer jeans to my home, such as it wasn't, with the painful tears that I didn't have, I watched the national news with my host family, in a language I didn't understand. I didn't understand the soil's tectonic betrayal, didn't understand that week's gang executions, in the same way I hadn't understood things in Northern Ireland, the way violence would squat in the air until the bombs showed up. I went to the Maximon shrine, bowing prayers to a cowboy-hatted mannequin in a Hefnered bathrobe, his fear-and-loathing Ray-Bans glinting rococo in a jeweled net of candles and rum bottles. I bowed to the Quecha woman sacrificing a chicken, bowed to the altar's tatted smoke of ashen candy and feathers, confessing to it the talismans of equanimity that didn't live inside my skin, how I could imagine being under the traitorous ground where there would be six dead children, each a brown-skinned poem nailed to nothing, the same color as the earth that had swallowed them. Not fair. Nothing fair. Not even fairness. Outside, tough-eyed kids kicked a soccer ball in the summer drizzle, missing their cousins. Their fathers wrapped rope around their waists, then lowered into the sinkholes. In the shadowed corner, a stack of mud-bloody baby clothes was ringed with clay figurines and feathers.

# HOME

Years ago, at a checkpoint in northwestern Ecuador,
    a soldier—nineteen, maybe—looked over my passport.
        He smelled of aftershave and sweat.

While we sweltered, waiting for the bomb-sniffing dogs,
    he talked of his cousin getting rich as a drywaller in Anaheim,
        asked what Corvettes sell for in los Estados Unidos,

and swiped through pictures of his family's village,
    showing us where he dreamed of someday
        building a small hacienda on a mountainside.

By now, he's probably ended up working for the narcos
    or drywalling in Anaheim, still scrolling through Corvette pictures
        and forever dreaming of his country home while never living there.

So much hungry swiping makes a joke of my need to lean
    on a tree and think. A lifetime of staring at AI-chosen screensavers
        of rustic cabins has birthed a nostalgia to sew myself into the soil,

to build shelters with trees I have cut, to stitch the earth
    with tubers to feed the children I want the future to be.
        It's an ancient need to speak in campfires and elk roasts,

to listen to the earth as an ancestor, even if
    this pulsing desire conveniently forgets that the tawny soil
        has often replied in famine or infant deaths.

Though we have irrefutably burned the boats
    on the way to this new world, we all dream of returning
        to our country home and yet we rarely do.

In Beijing, countless people —living shoulder to smog with twenty million others—
    tearfully sang John Denver's "Take Me Home, Country Roads."
        Or that time when I sang "My Tennessee Mountain Home" in a Tampa arena,

with thirty thousand dentists and off-duty air force lieutenants,
    housewives and Afghan refugees, before we all gridlocked our way
        to duplexes and air-conditioned dreams of prehistoric, limbic Edens.

Have you ever felt the bones inside your bones call out to a patch of earth
    and then not acted on it?  Me neither, and what does that
        unanswered dream banging around your soul do to you?

# REFUGE

As permafrost softened
and parts per million surged
and lawyers circled the oil rigs,
I followed the ancient hoof grooves
across the tundra, stumbling over tussocks
in a small city of caribou, through the huntings
of wolves and the sunblind grizzlies and three-day-old
wobbling calves, and went deep, wherever that was, into
the hard calloused body that ancestors lived inside, into migrations
across land where bones were broken and fires mysterious and priorities
failed and politics failed and there was only the big, raw, hard unrelenting earth.
The nightless, treeless, arctic landscape was part cave painting and part slushy taiga
calamitous feedback loop of the collapsing thermodynamic vault that was existential threat.
A thousand miles west of my monkish truancy, an obsessed scientist was gathering reindeer.
Herding musk oxen. Bison and wild horse hooves regrassed Beringia to lock in carbon,
with rusty Soviet tanks mimicking ten-ton mammoth trample to deepen the once
permanent underturf freeze. There were Harvard geneticists shaping elephant
helices into a mammothish fetus inside a birthing tank, the first of a herd.
Was the gulag ark a Jurassic punchline or a better bet than seeding
the atmosphere with aerosols? The ravenous microbial swarm
hung heavy with mosquitoes, grant money and cold-resistant
hemoglobin. Between the deep past and the future, a man
sits in a grassy valley. Pleistostalgia or futureproofing?
The answer grazes the hot, wet stomachs of large
herbivores and the collapsing sinkholes of taiga.
The earth forgives itself for the long valleys
of drought, the axes of ice, the windows
of biotic flourishing and scarcity,
the shifts. Now the deep past.
Now the narrow passage
to the deep future.
The now is long.

# GEOTRAUMATICS

High in the Arctic,
I ran into a reality-TV film crew
huddled in the wind while they waited
for the next bush plane back to available WiFi.
They had a celebrity activist with them who was almost
as famous for championing the wild as for hitting his ex-girlfriend.
As a friend once said, "It's hella' lot easier to love a tree than a person,"
but his wilderness-as-therapy ended in suicide. I talked with the crew for a few
minutes before setting out to follow the ten thousand caribou that were migrating
across the valley as they have for thousands of years, centering the whole ecosystem.
Which may stop soon if Exxon drills for oil in their millennial birthing grounds.
Mountains are full of broken people running and climbing and hiking away
from traumas. I'm still waiting to hear back from the famous kayaker
who got excited about removing dams for a hot minute before his
Instagram account went back to hucking waterfalls and drinking
craft beer. But such are the problems of the age, now that
we don't have to outrun world war. Now I can follow
caribou across a mountain range for weeks, alone:
an ancient story, and yet such a modern thing
to do. I can rejoice in seeing no humans.
And what does that say about me?

## UGGIANAQTUQ

And so the polar bear became a Patagonia campaign, a Sierra Club calendar photo, a YouTube video on which so many clicked the sad emoji. A victory for branding but not ultimately for the bear. The endless drift of extinction. Can you imagine your world literally melting away? My Inuit friends in Alaska had a word: *Uggia-naqtuq*, "to behave strangely,"—of the weather, how the dispersing cloud foretells a storm that comes in minutes instead of a day, the way spring is born again and again with melting, thawing, metling, thawing. The polar bear and I are born -again as globalized citizens. The great white gods refugee their way south as the brown and black people head north, and the white people argue over what to do. Once a god of the mysterious barren north, you're now a disoriented beggar seeing trees for the first time. Cruise ships. Exxon waits in the wings. Who could care as you wander a highway in Newfoundland, far from your beloved ice? I'm thinking about booking a luxury cruise through the Northwest Passage, to see it all before it's gone. I'm hoping to see a polar bear, but not too close.

# SUBTERRANEAN

He crawled in the musty tunnel,
a nervous breathing shouldering
through an inky nothing, startled
by his own unrelenting heartbeat.
As the tour guide talked of how
the Viet Cong had lived underground
for years, he imagined them growing
more earth-like, as U.S. fighter jets
must have seemed sky-like. For years,
while spading his yard to plant trees,
he'd thought of all of those soldiers
and grandmothers and kids digging,
but whereas he stopped in six minutes
to plunk in an organic, tended sapling,
they didn't stop for two fierce decades,
and then it was a year later and this
black walnut was growing while that
platoon had been bloodily halved.
In Da Nang, last year's rickety bridges
had been replaced overnight,
with LEDs pulsing, gleaming, cable stays
and dragons spewing fire on the hour.
The skyline was a big-shouldered mob
of high rises, glassy and urgent,
that rebuked the sky while chickens
pecked scooter-packed streets below.
It felt like nothing he would tell his wife
that night, on the phone across twelve
time zones. She'd ask about the trip.
As if. They would decide, that night,
after a winter's sinking struggle,

that their marriage was over
and he didn't know what else to say.
"This place is crazier every year," he said.
As they started to talk of apartments
and selling their acreage of fruit trees,
black birds erupted from his chest.
Hanging up, he stepped out into
the sweltering night, a new animal
blinking at an incomprehensible moon.

# BALLAD OF THE DOPAMINURGIC MONKEY

What a crazy endeavor, these half-million years
of evolving an absurdly big brain inside a relatively
hairless body with opposable thumbs and glutes
for walking upright and hips for birthing babies
with big heads to hold the big brain that tries to
manage prehistoric instincts as algorithms rain down
harder everyday from the incomprehensible cloud.
You wake up and scratch yourself and pee and walk
the dog, feeling the cold earth under your not-quite
prehensile bare feet, and check your email and drink
coffee and fart, putting yourself in front of one screen
after another, checking other screens, always checking
and clicking and seeking until you stop to roll around
with your dog or look at the sky with your daughter,
the same sky that other hominid species gazed at
a hundred thousand years ago, the same yearning clouds
that will whisper of this spinning planet a century or ten
from now to the machines that will remember us like
Neanderthals or passenger pigeons or medieval people
who were always drunk because the water wasn't safe:
We will be folksongs and footnotes to them,
like Robin Hood or the land bridge, or the great flood.
They'll marvel at how we kept searching and hungering
and loving and fighting until we evolved ourselves
out of the water, out of the trees, out of tails, out of
the forest, out of existence, into a new world where our
semi-digi-descendents will be spared peeing and fucking
and coffee and child-bearing hips, the craving and seeking
and the story of this sweating, grunting wondrous life
that each day will get harder and harder to call human.

# EVENING WITH ED

When I'm wincing in that so-lonesome-I-could-cry kind of way,
I can always skulk around some construction site,
on the backfilled edge of a wetland, home to a future Target.

Thinking of the red-winged blackbirds that will never skim these acres,
I hack flagging tape, jounce thoughtfully surveyed stakes
out of the gouged fill, padlock the dozer door against twilight's purpling.

I think of Ed Abbey, that tall tequila chug of cantankerous rants,
back in the seventies, chainsawing some billboard on Tucson's dusty outskirts,
one shot of saint and two of 12-gauge, kissed with a sprig of joyful lust.

A fox scurries under the site trailer as cackles of blackflies drift
heat's fading. What last week were beavers and dragonflies,
is now gravel desert as plundered as Peshawar's craters.

Abbey, in another desert across the world, stood in a complex arroyo
of lewd grace. But he did stand. Yet here, in the morning, forty men will arrive,
ready to turn earth into commerce. Cowbirds loiter over stacks of girders.

Five hundred feet to the west is an archive of ferns, turtles and herons;
to the east the smooth orphaned ether of evening's commute.
As my compass needle wobbles inside the contradictions, I kick

a stolen spade weakly and wonder what Ed thought in the quiet
twilight moments, without an audience or writerly ambition.
What hope he held for his charred soul. What hope I hold for mine.

# HACKED ANIMAL

As cytokine backed us into the future, I locked down,
lax as a blanket and stymied, left to putter and veer.
Each screenworn day slumped into the same nowhere
—all droplets and superstition, boredom and bleating—
while the dusty brahmins, bankrupt with legacy,
locked and hoarded their last stand, pretending
that the sea of anxiety wasn't deeper and stormier.

But my cave glands knew that the digital intimacies
were a false-ish balm, a glitchy lifeboat in reality's
shattered prism. Pulped-up and sulky, I crutched
yet deeper into data's snazzy marinade, doing my best
to skirt the strafing ultimatums—the fraying weather
and puckering agencies, the mercantile mudslide—
even as consequences called in oversold IOUs.

I'd been backed into a corner, or at least a cloud server,
but transcending my shoe-purchase history and sleep data
would require going beyond the screen's frictionless
oblivion. Would I birth a scarred-up resurrection?
Straining against a dwindling attention span, I ached
heavy as a hungry ghost, trying to rummage a new credo.
Redeem the unredeemable? Maybe not. But even as
the wound swelled, I had to figure out a way through.

# WALLED GARDEN

These people are protecting bison and sage grouse
and grassland ecosystems. Non-profiting up patchworks
of land for this land trust or that park or that owl.

Lobbying to keep this forest roadless or to protect those
wolves, or save someone's children from digital depression.
These people are demanding to delist those grizzlies,

to sell off that wildlife refuge, to buy those mining rights.
They are swinging hammers of money and protest to make
more money to not lose money to keep family together.

They are killing wolves to keep cattle, to hold values.
These people are crowded on benches, on their iphones,
waiting for Old Faithful to erupt on the hour, killing time

watching David Attenborough shows in the walled garden
that is Netflix, in the walled garden that is Yellowstone,
in the walled garden that is the United States.

They are entering passwords to check the price of wolf
t-shirts on Amazon Prime compared to the park gift shop.
They are taking pictures, taking videos, measuring steps,

posting all of it to a cloud that knows them better
than they know themselves. These people are hunched
and sunburned in the desert as they hide from border patrol

who find them with satellites, as javelina grunt past them
as GPS-tracked Grizzlies grunt across Yellowstone's
park boundary, one minute protected, the next not,

migrating toward extinction, that burned-down church
that is all wall and no garden. I'm swiping through bear
and wolf pictures on my phone, a clumsy civilized effort

to give wild oxygen to my choked biology, and wondering
if we love things more when they're scarce, especially when
there's this foreground filter bubble of distraction, not in the

bison or sage grouse but burrowing inside people who are staving
off boredom and trolling but mostly working hard to keep their corner
of the garden growing while the weather gets more intense.

A strange recipe: two parts mammal gland instincts
with one part binge -clicking and one part culture, and you get
the only creatures who actually cultivate gardens even as

we destroy them, even as constantly refreshing this or that app
walls off our own interior gardens, all of which are complicated
responses to the knowledge of the garden that we originally
came from and are mostly failing to find our way back to.

# GREENLAND

For James Altucher

I've decided to buy Greenland. It's lonely, cold and melting, a problem to be solved.
Just look at a map and you'll see an island the size of Saudi Arabia with a population
the size of Dubuque, Iowa. Its ice caps are melting and making weather unstable for
the rest of us. Passed by in the global economy, it has a GDP lower than Lesotho's.
It is simply silence in the great white north. A hunk of unused rock where a handful
of Danish semi-citizens huddle under the endless arctic night like anchorites, eating
salted fish and watching Scandinavian crime dramas. So. I can buy with an easy
mind. But who even does that? Maybe I can hire an exponential life coach or start
a #buygreenland social media movement or partner with a Chinese startup to take
it over for ski resort rights, except that a few Tibetans and Taiwanese have warned
me how those kinds of deals tend to turn out. Nevertheless, Greenland deserves a
better future. We'll 3D–print carbon-negative cities with vertical gardens that grow
five-hundred pound cabbages in the twenty-four hour summer, so much closer to
utopia than the perennially dysfunctional Costa Rican ecovillages. We all must wake
up each morning, so why not do it creatively? Should I hire Inuits to guide ecotour-
ists on aurora borealis dogsled tours? Could we corner the market as the last place
to see a wild polar bear? Wouldn't the robotized mining operations be elegant and
free of human rights problems? Isn't this a logical precedent to life on Mars? No. We
come from the earth and we must keep our feet planted within the relentless gravity
of our lives. Perhaps I'll Kickstarter this enterprise, offer up tax havens and vacation
home plots to survivalists and billionaires. Would AIs be interested in the first na-
tion with robot citizenship? The massive island shrugs off more ice and settles into
its tectonic plates. A frontier under a frontier. It's a narwhal in a goldfish world. The
ten-thousand-pound Mercator-distorted gorilla on the top of this spinning planet.
Its glaciers penetrate the imagination. Canada and Russia are too busy fighting over
Arctic shipping lanes to bother. How to proceed? On Monday morning, I'll reach
out to Queen Margrethe II of Denmark. I will talk of the spirit of her Viking an-
cestors and offer her rare-earth mineral rights, the first refusal rights to the Netflix
series about Knud Rasmussen, a sea-steading compound outside of Nuugaatsiaq. In
its own dowdy, cold, northern way the island mumbles *develop me, develop me.*

# DISTANCE

If only I spoke mesquite or jacaranda.
Under the pelt-thick weight of this earth
I lean on a crumbling wall sipping mescal,
mumbling stories and shrugging off midnight's
sudden uprising of air horns and fireworks.
The scribble of sounds not quite the same
as the rattle of police machine guns or her
sleeping breath on my face or the stray dog
running toward me.  In the Sierra Norte,
along a washboard road, we met a banker
trying to explain economic zones to campesinos.
On Avenida Benito Juarez, Zapotec women nursed
their children while selling carved jaguars
and next year's calendars decorated with Frida Kahlo.
In the morning we will walk past sunburned men
patching adobe twenty feet up on rickety ladders.
Over the crumbling walls, they will mix mud and lean
and stretch and patch further and further out,
trying to rebuild earth on top of the earth.

# EMPIRE

Staggering, daffy at 11,000 feet, he notes to himself that
Trip Advisor doesn't give a ranking to Francisco Pizarro,
who said cuddly things like "Prepare your hearts as a fortress,
for there will be no other," before being stabbed in the throat.

Nor does it give a ranking to Tupac Amaru, who was beheaded
in 1572, before a cheering crowd, a few Lonely Planet feet from
a blue-haired Quechua guy who is trying to sell weed to tourists.
Dusk's harsh light rasps the stubbled mountains. Cusco.

Lightheaded, he walks canyonish alleys up the cliffsides,
through a thousand years of Inca-slaved masonry propping up
five centuries of Spanish stucco, now occupied by North Face franchises
and Starbucks and Ayahuasca tour companies, all Instagram linked.

He guesses that Atahualpa never imagined his empire would collapse
at the speed of sound, never imagined that the spoils of eternity
would become a UNESCO brand, all gawk and New Age reverence
and alpaca sweaters, tidily marketed in four-day Sacred Valley packages.

*There are desires to not disappear and there are desires to die,*
*fought by two opposing waters that have never isthmused,* wrote Vallejo.
And these haunted streets, thumped by ten thousand ambitions,
it seems to him, are a monument to desire, just like the narcotrafficantes

down the Urubamba Valley steadily moving desire up to Juarez,
like the Chinese mining companies up in Cajamarca are feeding desire
for cadmium so tourists can check Trip Advisor on their new iPhones.
He thinks of the women who have prayed for death in these streets,

because of the desire of men who were rummed-up, oafish, and throbbing,
or just following orders. That night he will dream that he is in the Plaza de Armas
and that all of the bodies of those who died violently in the past
seven hundred years are piled into a mountain higher than any of the Andes.

# THE RUSTLING FORGE

A mountain lion sleeps up-range
of the 101's halogened decibels,
      above the sunken red crags of twilight rooftops.


      The lion is wilder than freeways,
less ancient than the San Andreas Fault, which is quaking
only a little according to the apps being tapped
          before drivers get off at exit 12A.
      The headlights' urgent parade
      stampedes beneath
the dusk's thousand gestures of bloody light.


          Downcanyon,
evening drapes the century-old ruins of an old zoo,
      all graffiti and picnic -tables,
as cars on the honking 101 drive past
the long-forgotten graves
          of camels and peacocks.


Across a golf course's dull turfy acres huddles a newer zoo,
      its choirs of tigers and giraffes dreamless in enclosures.
A hunger sculpted from a hundred thousand years of hunting
          rises like a fire through the puma's stomach
            though the manzanita is gauzy with smog.
        Sinewed paws crunch the xeric stubble,
      passing brittlebush and gnatcatchers.


      This driver,
swiping, merging through the syntax of concrete,
has dumbed down the hills' trophic hardness—
      that mule deer's

frantic repose, half-grazing and preyish
within a mile of its own zoo-cloistered kind.
     The lion saunters,
radio-collared, pinging waypoints
across the evening's vague astronomy
     to satellites back to mainframes, dropping breadcrumbs of wildness
in the warming oven I have sought to escape my entire life.

     This rosy boa
coils under antennae coil toward the starlight
that has forgotten its name across six years
of steering into our distracted eyes.
     Lion maps the darkness,
the earth graceful in her anchorite feet.

     Across the endless city
of gusting light and urgency, hidden thousands
     are breathing hush back into moments,
     breathing lament into dancing with awe,
     breathing electricities across their impulses
     to breathe their loneliness
to the pure spaces on the other side of the stars.

     Wolves and bighorn sheep and antelope
keep escaping from the zoo like they miss
the lion, who is hunting on the other side of freedom.
     For moments or days
     they churn the full throat of their instincts
     in the rustling forge of bone and thirst and combat.

Joan of Arc     Harriet Tubman     Geronimo
     were doing the same thing.

# PLAZA DEL TOROS

No shit or blood. Just the relentless, blinding sun. In the halls of the arena, all of
those massive horned heads mounted on well-scrubbed walls. Families from Dubai
and Topeka snapping selfies in front of Goya etchings and bronze sculptures,
but no shit or blood. Only Gibraltarish heat frying my brainpan: a scramble of
Hemingway's pontificating and my fifth-grade self being chased across a mucky
pasture by the neighbor's bull. The ground rumbles with a dozen dark animals as
the sky rings with cathedral bells, and I stagger, unable to find my querencia. Is it
the auroch, archaic in my brain stem, that unfastens my balance? Is it because this
whole pageant is as pristine as the Tokyo Museum's death-notched katanas?
As Franco surely knew, it ain't all pizzazz and sequins. Such blood no cape can cover
up. A botched abdomen? The interregnum between beauty and horror? In air-
conditioned offices and cafés across Seville, millennial scrutineers mock the torero,
a dusty relic of a million years of hunting, a penance tasting unnecessarily of blood.
No one said it's easy being a minotaur in a virtual world. Maybe Ernest thought
of this when he tasted the cold metal of his shotgun, realizing he'd been forged on
a different anvil than he'd thought. But regardless, the monster behind the gate
stomps the earth. The crowd roars.

# TERMINAL VELOCITY

Could it be construed as illiberal
or the curse of the occult?
What sauntered on surfaces and breezes was
        neither partisan nor crude.
In that remorseless air, our shared destiny
had gone all cockeyed, detoured by masks,
shifting goalposts, and gotchas.
        I refused to knuckle under,
but, knee-deep in distraction, couldn't help
watching #yetanotherviralfiasCOVIDeo
as its algorithms watched me back.
        I was as flattened as a curve,
as slumped as the S&P, just another handwasher
hypnotized by the Groundhog Day that left all of us
sulky at the end of the end of history:
        I want a haircut! I deserve to eat out!
Left to hoard Charmin, scuttle up the WiFi
bandwidth, and scoff at gunned-up protesters,
we stay-at-homed like pros, nervy and bored.
        The virus went looking for its appetite
in meatpacking plants and hospital corridors,
dancing on blood sugars and swollen artery walls
until not-only-elders evaporated to fly off
        in the shape of the druthers we didn't have,
on unused flight paths above unsmogged cities.
The willingness to change was the x
we were solving for over a denominator of anguish.
        Yet, the drift and cloy of the strung-along days
—so far from the emergency's distant croon—
kept me from running midnight to dawn on my knees.

Not quite guileless, I was left to despair
        over the mediocre vaudeville of halfassed -distancing,
Zoom calls, minor league Armageddon,
the glaze of hysteria, as passively as any schmuck.

# ARANYANI

Our purple-haired waitress has a forearm tattoo of Aranyani,
the Hindu forest deity, and we're talking migration corridors,
desert tortoises and rewilding over Onokoroshi and Tuna Tataki
while next to us a group of brogrammers are talking AI, betting
on how long before the bots take over. I'm eight years old again
in Central Maine's forests, contemplating yet another Moose
while coveting the $29.99 Radio Shack robot in the Sunday flier.
The code ninjas are hoodies and apportunity while the tree
huggers are Marin cool and well-stocked wine cellars. We joke over
reintroduced grizzlies roughing up Shasta crystal shops and they
dude-chortle about a VC youtube video that went viral.

     And here's another joke that really happened in 1893:
Muir, Tesla, and Kipling walk into a bar-a dinner party, actually-
Tesla explaining how he'll hydroelectrify Niagara Falls. Muir sniffs
disdainfully at this incursion into the wild, and Kipling makes a joke
about how the future has Muir over a barrel, going down the falls,
and here we are a century later, still kegging down Niagara's gush.
Maybe the AIs will move us into a post-carbon utopia, or maybe
they'll pass over humans in favor of a functioning gulf stream
and swallow migrations. Or maybe carbon levels hockeystick
and the barrel crashes in a symphony of refugees and starvation.
As the techies update their instragrams and the conservationists
drive their Teslas back across the bay to Sausalito, I wonder:
Has Aranyani lived through these dimensions before,
or is this some new velocity and what are we hurtling towards?

# PANDEMIC

*In the distance, form includes the Great Void, heaven and earth,*
*mountains and rivers and forests. Nearby, it includes this body of flesh*
*and blood that appears before us.*
   —Chen-k'o, 1595


We are told to mask, even as our leaders refuse.
The screaming protesters think their AR-15s
will protect them from the virus,
   a medieval supposition,
but then again Hui-Neng wrote the Platform Sutra
in the seventh century, a wisdom we have yet
   to catch back up to.
Closing is opening and opening is closing
is doublespeak is a koan is the reason
I am deep in the Maine woods
   where there are no people,
even if every year there are more ticks that will
dismantle my body down to rotting studs.
   I am scratched and lost and happy
in the one place where frictionless ecommerce
isn't mining my subconscious, even as I slap
at clouds of blackflies unfastening dark riverbeds of blood.
Bugs. In the jungle outside Iquitos I sweltered,
mudfooted and bitten, groggy with the density of life.
Wrist-sore from coring trees
   to measure drought from tree rings,
I talked in grants and isotopes
while the Ribereños slashed hectares and smoked,
   tinkering at coughing engines.

In nearby Belén, the floating market was a lathering stink
of alligator heads, hacked-up snakes,
         monkeys sweating on tables.
Under the thick-aired sun,
fresh-from-the-jungle Ayahuascanauts
stepped past hog-sized fish sulking in tubs
to dally over jaguar claw necklaces before flying home
to Stuttgart and St. Louis,
         misted with the same yawning microbes
that float in the oil-and-rubber-filled container ships
chugging down the muddy Amazon toward Manaus.
              Somewhere a thousand immigrants
wade deep inside my bloodstream with half-feral
         adaptation,
carrying the jungle inside me,
         hacked and burned and planted.
They ask me what I will do with the rest of my life
and I do not know.  I must find my original face
         before the algorithms assign it to me.

# DU FU

Jet-lagged in a Chengdu tea house, you're finally willing to admit that
      your poems have failed to change the world.
Words that once aspired to thieve fire now dawdle at the back of the bus,
      lesser than clickbait. And there he sits,
Du Fu, across bustling tables of pu-erh, across centuries, destitute as coal.
      You think you know how he feels, eyes agonied
at the sky's prosperous asbestos fog, or maybe at memories of flaming arrows
      driving fire into alleys, war carts and horses punishing the streets.
Trade tariffs and cyberwarfare have nothing on blood-moaning ditches,
      body-strewn streets. Or take this honking, scootered street,
where freshly detonated building rubble smokes, soon to be Uniqlo and Forever 21.
      Take your spiky-haired tablemate answering call
after call, leveraging a mining deal in Tibet, lining up a Yangtze dye factory.
      talking Ugandan water rights as he shifts selvedge-jeaned legs,
spinning a hard-gleamed Omega on his wrist. Take Chang'an, a thousand dusty
      winters ago: smoke growing in the mouths of the dead,
children starving.  Take all the examples of what we have all done during
      these rudderless times.  So what to do?
You could nail your heart to the hard planks of the past—crouching, observant
      and armored. You could strike out for your small tribe,
guarding a pile of all you find. You could rage against this ten-thousand-year-old
      churn of fire. You could live a quiet life.
You could spend a lifetime searching the tawny margins until one night you find
      yourself tumbling in some great, dark-bellied sea.
In that battering chaos, your longing senses a dozen unruly breathings nearby,
      fierce-eyed and wild.  Slowly, you are getting closer.

# GEOENGINEERING

When
hope seems
to be dwindling,
I can always graft
some water onto ice
to build a frozen stupa
that will mimic a glacier
to provide meltwater
for a village in the dry months.
I can lug tubing up the mountain into
a north-facing valley to harness the donations
of the sky into an ice cone that I will bow to,
less for dharma and more for survival.
Or I can help roll concrete balls into the ocean to rebuild reefs.
Or use drones, programmed to replant forest with specific biodiversity.
Maybe this will mean fewer space sunshades and injecting aerosols into
the atmosphere, but probably not. When the earth turns itself inside out,
you can never go home again, even if you never left. This occurred to me in a
Berklee conference room, as three tenurers with no skin in the game prattled
on about solastalgia, that sense of psychic or existential distress over ecolog-
ical change. They proposed giving up the white privilege of Muir's spiritual
solitude and instead measuring our relationship to the earth in terms of cli-
mate refugees and carbon taxes. Which felt like writing lovemaking poems
in terms of spermatozoal emission. So how to chase beauty in the newsfeed
of tragedy? Make mandalas of microplastics circling in the North Pacific?
Genomically de-extinct the passenger pigeon to resuscitate ecosystems?
Dizzy with isms, I start back up the mountain, careful to step lightly on the
melting glacier, a future inside a crevasse inside an opportunity inside a loss.

# HACKABLE ANIMAL

*For Yuval Noah Harari*

Ah! To be alive on a mid-August morn, fording a silty stream,
        barefoot, breath steaming, North Cascades,
Kulshan's white massif at back, staring up hacked-out granite
        at a radio collared mountain goat staring down,
a shaggy silence in the pitching vault of the sky. Almost certainly
        he was flown here from Olympic National Park,
a century after his ancestors were trapped and trucked from here
        to there. Brother goat, I wonder at last year's airlift,
as you and so many others swung blue-blindfolded and sedated,
        orange-harnessed in open air, helicoptered
across Puget Sound, as we watched the KING-TV livestream.
        All to preserve wildness by moving wildness
to less wild places to make them more wild places, which is to say,
        we're working pretty hard at the preservation
of the world, preserving goats in parks along with silence,
        preserving wild places in parks and on screens,
taking screens into wild places in place of silence and mystery,
        putting on collars and monitors and screens
to track data and heartrate and attention and sleep to help me
        and the goat and the alpine ecosystem to upgrade
our downgraded autonomies, each of us a wilderness becoming a park.

# EXPONENTIAL

Not speak out of both sides of my destiny, but hell no,
I won't crave or spurn the singularity, nor fetishize
metaconnectivity, even as my brainstem anxiousizes into
a slow burn of robots and Armageddon. Even if the gods
burrowing in the wild garlic have all gone awry.
If I'm only an outdated artifact, roving far from the lab—
sweating in the tilth, shouting at the sun, passed over
by the quants and early adopters who crowbar possibility
and moonshot connectivity among the yoked and titillated—
then I'll be a muddled bard, pawing tree bark's mossy braille,
mumbling, and chivvying myth like a broken-down anchorite.
And the starting-to-flicker of that once-bedrock fact—
that we all die—has me moshed up inside like an overripe
musk melon, wobbly, splotched and passed over.
Fess up: Do we know if we need death to say what our years
have meant to the curvature of time? Or what makes us human?
The love and fuck? The yawnish hours? The alchemical brooding
of the blues, the fears I've carried in my creel— all of it has me
feeble in my skin. I gape at the moment's sheer velocity,
hoping to coax the hint of a sign, a gobble of initiation,
a true convergence. What emerges, what disappears.

# EDM

LEDs, MDMA. TR-808s and 120 BPM.
A Bogota DJ shifting trap beats, popping bass drops,
triple-timing hi hats-three against two, the dubbed-out heartbeat
of icaros chants frenzying the psytrance, the pitched-down vocals soaring
over bass wobble, hyping, hyping, remixing microgenres or hardstyling
kinetic breaths of content creators, eports teams and coders,
until we all floated into a dopamined equilibrium.

All the jungle around us a chlorophylled utopia
so not the ads of carbon-neutral and waste-free, not the beauty
of the pinwheeling light installations, not the epiphanies and friendship bands.
It was trances broken by overdoses and kids jetting in from Miami, funk hunting
and hypno-vaping, theta waves edging toward gamma in the deep now.
The bass house trances amped into breath sessions and acrobatics
that sought to manifest, dyeing our neuroreceptors
in empathy's lucid grace.

Dub squads and magic hugs. We painted our names
in the sky. We sobbed at the borealis of rippling lasers. As much as
we aspired to third eye, the stars nailed to our souls were a little too glitzy,
a little too easy. A thousand BassBoss speakers bellowed the inheritance of
our culture reaching, getting claimed by a new world, with kettlebelled abs
and Yeezyness, watching ourselves on the live feed from the
drone above: the shifting, colored tide of bodies,
desperate to behold.

"Give me release, let the waves of time and space
surround me," we sang to the dancing muses in furry boots,
to the pure spaces to accept our offerings, to give the deep earth seven prayers
and a dream. We rode the wounded pulses, even as entrance
to the sun was blocked, hoping to find
the other side.

# MASTERMIND

That night, the sky fickle with stalled wind,
he was invited to join a transformational mastermind
where he'd learn to be a wealthy bodhisattva
warrior poet with a fully realized microbiome.

He'd swing kettlebells and ketamine in Tulum
and Sedona. Part shamanic journeys and part
investment workshops that would fast-track
enlightenment. Bathed in neurofeedback,

he'd upgrade his internal life for a mere
$20,000, roughly the cost of installing
a series of village water purification systems
in the unglittered Yucatan dustiness.

Was this really how he would be guided to serve?
He wondered how brainhacking compared
to what Bodhidharma saw, staring at the cave wall
for nine years, what Mandelstam dreamed of,

starving in Vladivostok. Underfoot, the earth
whispered dioramas of it-could-happen into
our ambitions. They crouched deep like prairie
grasses ready to spring. The Nigerian oil well

could be a hundred-year hurricane, the Gobi
solar array a recovered Montana grizzly.
Feeling history's elbow on his throat, he
couldn't but help sense a sham, a pit of skulls.

Were we to forfeit yet another glacier for our transcontinental ayahuasca journey? He kept staring at the cave wall. He prayed he wouldn't need to cut off his eyelids to stay awake.

# BEAUTIFUL REBELLION
*for Ana Tijoux*

"We will triumph," Victor Jara said, his guitar fingers broken before
he was riddled with forty bullets, one for each year of his life.

The gun to Violetta Parra's head was held by her own hand,
as shaky  in that moment as it had once been strong, strumming.

*Few of us can be expected to be perfectly integrated*
*in this disintegrating world*, I think, high in the thin air

of the Ecuadorian cordillera, as patchy Internet pulls in
reports of a hemisphere tear-gassed with desperation,

as dissenters joust and ebb from Caracas to Punta Arenas,
dogfighting and wrangling across the barrios and calles.

Women are deploying their bodies across Spanish plazas
slave-laid by their indigena ancestors. The pot-banging fracas

of Concepcion's cacerolazo protest marches in the defiant,
tragic footsteps of Victor and Violetta, injected with

a techish, clickbait momentum, distilled into
the sleeker now of Ana Tijoux's horn-heavy rebel music.

And as I, half norteamericano, half exilized globaler,
hunker, dilettantish, on this end of the American experiment,

I'm thinking of Ana's hip hop, its swaggering defiance
full of charango and bolero, the brassy NYC street beats

underlying the jazzy, exacting flow that battles sirens
as they speak of subway fare in Santiago and cerrado fires

in São Paulo. Beats that boast in Mapuche and wiphala flags,
unshaken by caudillo socialism and rubber bullets.

Beats that know Bogota y Lima, that crouch in smoky
Aymara villages and wince at the Yanacocha mines

and body-filled FARC valleys. Beats born in Pinochet exile
that tell of throwing stones at la policia de Quito

while Moreno and his ministers hide in Guayaquil,
their money hiding in Cayman Island tax havens.

And now, Ana, you're the same age as Bolivar at his peak
when he was uniting much of the continent away from Madrid

at the bloodiest possible price. El Libertador was unhorsed
by his own violent legacy within a year, but you'll keep

plowing the sea, MC, *a mujer fuerte insurgente* in a world
cut in half, guns crouching over open veins on one side,

grandmothers with eyes quiet as jaguars on the other.
We're in the New World after all, right? Maybe it's time

for less Che, more Mama. "Break the chains of the indifferent,"
you say. "La hora sono," you sing. The time has come.

# FOUNTAIN OF TEARS

Wherever there was water,
      we followed the two-thousand-year-old flow.
           We drank.
           The Romans, the Umayyad,
           caliphate and Berber.
             Falangista and entrepreneur.
           Built and rebuilt aqueducts and terrazas:
     walls upon walls upon fortresses
   upon mosques upon tiles upon brick
upon stone upon mortar around the beveled rain,
the snowmelt to ditches
to gutters to fields.
The black-toothed Roma and the Moor-sired Spaniard
       held each other until they were red
          against the whitewashed walls
            of the sunbaked brown hills.


          On a million blazing afternoons, we bowed
our lips to any indent in the rock, any gush or dribble,
blood or oil or agua. We drank from the Koran,
      the Sephardic Talmud, the Reina-Valera Bible,
         the hanging hocks of hogs that we hacked and peeled,
         the distant herds
of sheep and goats, the ibex and boar.


                  We were a flood of inquisitions
and revolts, droughts of heretics and expulsion. Vectors for burning
     at the stake and conversion. We sipped from el sangre de mudejars,
      swallowed like priests the swords of immigration. The first Spanish republic
        was the last glacier.
          The civil war was trading Machado and García Lorca

for bullet gouges in brick.
Franco was repression and isolation,
  los granjeros abandoning olive groves for work in Madrid factories.
  Water working its rosary in the millenniumed firehose of human traffic.
Water the central tenant of blood.
Water gulped from discarded bottles
  by Guineans and Algerians whose thirst for water
   had crossed saltwater to find tarped pallets of EU water
  in overfull Malaga refugee camps.
Water in a thousand-year-old fountain where García Lorca was shot
  after midnight by firing squad.
  Before his head hit the earth,
  his blood was already sinking
  into the earth, seeking water,
   returning
    to its own
     kind.

# BRACE FOR IMPACT

The pop-up ad said something about
saving our oceans, which seemed as useless
as vape package health warnings.
Empathy is hard when your aperture
is twelve thousand miles wide
and the focus button is broken.
      "What does it smell like?" I ask.
"Did my grandfather take me fishing there?
When I was nineteen did I sneak over a fence
with my girlfriend and make love
with the sound of high tide crashing
against my sand-etched knees
while the Milky Way whirled above our bodies?"
      Across the emptyish parking lot,
surfers mildewed into wetsuits, twisted
at rusty zippers, waxed chapped fiberglass.
I monkeyfisted into the gushing foam until
the kayak floated and the paddle caught froth.
The horizon hiding behind towering avalanches
of boom and breakers. Crush and wash and roll.
Ice cream headaches and ears full of sand.
      So not the Insta posts of Banzai Pipeline
nor the Gidgety rhapsodies of Orange County skin.
It was numb hands and squints interrupted
by facefuls of icy Atlantic. Brace and surge,
scurrying between wave troughs to not be
crushed by walls of Greenland salt.
Prehistoric instinct and shivers.
      I calligraphed the green gray sea
with a paddle, hustling like a prizefighter.

Wiped snot. As much as catching waves,
I was Saint Brendan trying to stay afloat.
Fool's errand or spiritual devotion?
I skidded down a wave until it pitched me
unbreathing under the great icy darkness.
Two thousand miles beyond this break,
glaciers the size of Manhattan were cracking off.

# IKKYU AT MESA VERDE

As high desert storm clouds close in, I stare into the musky sky,
searching for the arroyo between an answer and a question,

forgetting that, like a downpour making a riot of a slot canyon,
the earth is simply earthing as I try to imagine the humaning

of all those who fucked and laughed and ground corn in these
pueblos for centuries before abandoning them to saltbush,

blue grama grass sagebrush, broom snakeweed, and ravens
during a drought that harvested starvation across decades.

The looming sky splatters on the page as I read Ikkyu's
*I hold my breath and listen to the dead singing under the grass,*

words written in the fifteenth century, not long before galleons
beached on this continent in their search for gold and slaves,

written a few centuries after these cliffs were abandoned
The hundreds of years between me kindling a fire and Ikkyu

and galleons and cliff-dwellers beating in each others' skulls
over scraps is only the blink of a rock,

just as the ancient Puebloans are staring up from under the loess,
and Teddy Roosevelt is staring down from the National Park signs,

from the geology exhibits, from the naturalists talking about
the current decades-long drought, from the policies protecting

cliff dwellings. Roosevelt, a weak boy inside a strong man inside
a fervent naturalist inside an imperialist, stares across the continent,

His bandelier-and-buckaroo statue charging ahead, virile,
as his barechested and noble sidekicks of color stare back.

Should we melt it down and return its minerals to the earth,
just as his Great White Fleet has surely rusted away to nothing?

Should we put it in a cemetery of our justly unhorsed white male icons?
Beside him, the Sierra Club will perch on Muir's granite headstone,

proclaiming each crack in his geologic firmament so that
their own early eugenics affiliations are forgiven.

People who haven't saved the Grand Canyon line up to point out
that Brower overlooked Black Mesa's coal development.

When the TR said to "leave it as it is," he conveniently failed
to include the continent full of people who had been smallpoxed,

shot and starved. But I suppose we all have our reservations.
Even if the Lakotas' are soaked with blood and poverty

and the Sierra Club's are structured in carefully worded tweets.
Even knowing that Mao and Lenin began by tearing down statues.

Put wilderness against colonialism against white supremacy
against commerce against the long now of evolution,

which simply lives and dies at the speed of adaptation.
But the panel of literary theorists debating about nature

as a social construct hasn't protected Yellowstone
as a biological island or inspired a century of conservation

or imagined a solution for digital privacy. And it is not nothing
that this isn't an overdeveloped Niagara Falls of hotels and casinos,

but it's also not nothing inside a something that this is the publicized
bone ground of someone's ancestors even as we live by burning fossils

and privatizing water and genes, pricing and quantifying until the earth
and humanity we don't share are gone and won't return our calls.

Until then, as long as forests and oceans are worth more dead
than alive, the siloed tribes will ransack each others' statues

while their genomes are edited, gigabitted and blockchained.
Our hunkering descendants will tear us down the same way

for tiptoeing around climate before we had to run from it.
Do the mirrors we hold up to ourselves show us what kind

of mirrors we are, as Ikkyu proposed?  The mosquitos buzz
and bite around my head, even though I'm squatting

above this smoky campfire in a spring drizzle, achy and flecked
with the gristly mud that we'll all one day return to.

# NOTES

### "CARBON IS THE OPENED HEART"
*Seasteaders* are startup communities that float on the ocean with strong political autonomy, separate from any nation.

### "PARAMO"
*Paramo* is a type of high-altitude grassland found in the Andes.
*Chimborazo, Cotopaxi* and *Cayambe* are volcanoes in Ecuador.

### "FIRE"
*Gifford Pinchot* was the founding head of the US Forest Service. His fire and conservation policies set the course for US forest management for much of the 20th century.

### "REINTRODUCTION"
*The Pittmann-Robertson Act*, passed in 1937, uses taxes on hunting weapons and ammunition to fund conservation and hunter education

### "CHANTEUSE":
*Concha Buika* is an Afro-Spanish singer known for flamenco and jazz.
*Buleria* is a type of flamenco rhythm or song.

### "MAXIMON"
Maximon is a Mayan deity and folk saint in the western highlands of Guatemala

### "EVENING WITH ED"
Ed Abbey was a 20th century American writer and activist who wrote ecologically-oriented books like *Desert Solitaire* and *The Monkeywrench Gang.*

### "DISTANCE"
Avenida Benito Juarez is a street in Oaxaca, Mexico.

## "EMPIRE"

*Francisco Pizarro* was a Spanish conquistador who was best known for the conquest of Peru.

*Tupac Amaru* was the last monarch of the neo-Inca state. After leading revolts against the Spanish, he was captured and executed.

*Cusco* is a city in the Peruvian Andes that was originally the center of the Incan Empire. It is the oldest city in the Americas.

*Atawalpa* was the last Incan emperor who was captured and killed by the Spanish in 1533.

Caeser Vallejo was a Peruvian poet in the early 20th century

*The Plaza de Armas* is the central square in Cusco. It was originally built by the Incans and then adapted by the Spanish.

## "PLAZA DEL TOROS"

*The Plaza del Toros* is the principle bull-fighting arena is Seville, Spain.

## "PANDEMIC":

*Hui-Neng* was a Buddhist monk in China who lived from 638-713. Known as the 6th Patriarch of Zen, he is best known for writing the Platform Sutra, once the central texts of Zen.

*Iquitos* is a city in the Peruvian Amazon. It is the biggest city in the world with no road access. It is famous for industry and transportation along the Amazon, and it is a popular base for tourists seeking psychedelic Ayahuasca experiences.

*Riberenos* are the inhabitants of the Amazon river-region. They generally have an ancestry that is a mix of Spanish and indigenous.

*Belen* is a shantytown on the outskirts of Iquitos, where people live in shacks on stilts above the river, and travel by canoe and motor boat. Belen had the biggest wet market in the Amazon until it was demolished by the government in 2020 during Covid.

## "DU FU"

*Du Fu* was a T'ang Dynasty poet. He is generally considered, along with Li Bai, to be the greatest poet in the history of China. Du Fu experienced extreme hardship during the An-Lu-Shan Rebellion, including the death of a child.

## "HACKABLE ANIMAL"

*Kulshan* is the traditional Lummi name for Mt Baker, the tallest mountain in Washington's North Cascades range.

*"EDM"*: TR808 is a type of drum machine commonly used in hip-hop and electronic music

*BPM* stands for beats-per-minute

## "MASTERMIND"

*Osip Mandelstam* was a 20th century Russian who died in exile in Siberia.

*Bodhidharma* was a 5th century monk who brought Zen to China from India. He famously sat facing a wall in a cave at the Shaolin monastery for nine years, cutting off his eyelids so he wouldn't fall asleep.

## "BEAUTIFUL REBELLION"

*Ana Tijoux* is a Chilean-French rapper and musician.

*Victor Jara* was a Chilean folk singer and activist who was tortured and killed during Agusto Pinochet's regime.

*Violeta Parra* was a Chilean musician, folklorist and ethnomusicologist who was known as "The Mother of Latin American Folk."

*Cacerolazo* is a form of protest which consists of a group banging on pots and pans to get attention.

*Charango* is a small Andean guitar-like instrument

*Bolero* is a slow genre of Latin music

*The Mapuche* are an indigenous group from southern Chile and Argentina

*Wiphala* is an emblem that represents all of the indigenous peoples of the Andes

## "FOUNTAIN OF TEARS"

*The Umayyad* was a Caliphate that ruled the Islamic world, including the Iberian peninsula, in the 8th century.

*The Berbers* are an ethnic group from North Africa.

## "IKKYU AT MESA VERDE"

*Ikkyu* was a 15th century iconoclastic Zen monk and poet.

# ACKNOWLEDGMENTS

I am grateful to the editors of the following publications in which a number of these poems first appeared:

*Deep Wild Journal:* "Refugia," "Geotraumatics," "Hackable Animal"

*High Desert Journal:* "Fire"

*Off the Coast:* "Kick," "The Narrow Road to the Interior," "Carbon is the Opened Heart"

*pacificREVIEW:* "Extinction," "Home," "Ballad of the Dopaminurgic Monkey"

*Writing for Peace:* "Distance," "Du Fu," "Empire"

I am deeply indebted to Baron Wormser, Dawn Potter, David Biespiel, Greg Glazner, Kevin Goodan, Juniper Moon, Sam Hamill, Gary Lawless, Kim Heacox, Sean Prentiss, and Stan Rubin for their inspiration, editorial assistance, generosity, mentorship, and belief in me as a poet.

## about the author

Ian Ramsey is a writer, educator and wilderness athlete based in Maine, where he directs the Kauffmann Program for Environmental Writing and Wilderness Exploration. His work has appeared in *Terrain.org*, *High Desert Journal*, and many other publications. Ian frequently leads expeditions and collaborates with climate scientists around North America and on other continents. He is a founding board member of Physiology First, a non-profit that gives cutting-edge tools to teens, families and educators to improve mental health and performance. In addition to teaching environmental topics, he teaches brain science, music and entrepreneurship for creatives. For more information, go to www.ianramsey.net

# WAYFARER

## BASED IN THE BERKSHIRE MOUNTAINS, MASS.

*The Wayfarer Magazine*. Since 2012, *The Wayfarer* has been offering literature, interviews, and art with the intention to inspires our readers, enrich their lives, and highlight the power for agency and change-making that each individual holds. By our definition, a wayfarer is one whose inner-compass is ever-oriented to truth, wisdom, healing, and beauty in their own wandering. *The Wayfarer's* mission as a publication is to foster a community of contemplative voices and provide readers with resources and perspectives that support them in their own journey.

**Wayfarer Books** is our newest imprint! After nearly 10 years in print, *The Wayfarer Magazine* is branching out from our magazine to become a full-fledged publishing house offering full-length works of eco-literature!

**Wayfarer Farm & Retreat** is our latest endeavor, springing up in the Berkshire Mountains of Massachusetts. Set to open to the public in 2025, the 15-acre retreat will offer workshops, farm-to-table dinners, off-grid retreat cabins, and artist residencies.

WWW.WAYFARERBOOKS.ORG

www.ingramcontent.com/pod-product-compliance
Lightning Source LLC
Chambersburg PA
CBHW052116020426

42335CB00021B/2790